PHOTOGRAPHER OF THE SOUTHWEST

ADAM CLARK VROMAN
1856-1916

Self-portrait taken at Isleta, N. M., 1899

PHOTOGRAPHER OF THE SOUTHWEST

Adam Clark Vroman, 1856-1916

EDITED BY RUTH I. MAHOOD

Curator Emeritus, History Division, Los Angeles County Museum
with the assistance of ROBERT A. WEINSTEIN

INTRODUCTION BY

BEAUMONT NEWHALL

Director, George Eastman House, Rochester

BONANZA BOOKS · NEW YORK

ACKNOWLEDGMENTS

ENCOURAGEMENT AND HELP HAVE come from many sources during the four years of research concerning Adam Clark Vroman and his work as a photographer. Members of the family, Mrs. Oscar Wiedmann and Mrs. Grace Wickersham, have shared family information with me. Library staffs have been most coöperative. These include the Los Angeles County Museum Library, the Pasadena Public Library, the University of California, Los Angeles, Library, the Los Angeles Public Library, and the Rockford (Illinois) Public Library.

Thanks and appreciation are due to all who have had a part in the progress of this work, especially to Dr. Lawrence Clark Powell whose perseverance discovered the long neglected negatives; to Mrs. Gladys Rorbaugh who first called them to my attention; to Miss Frieda Fall who carefully copied the original negative inventory; to Mr. Glen Dawson at whose suggestion this book was considered; to Mr. Carl Dentzel, Director, The Southwest Museum, for generously making available the full facilities of the Musuem, including the use of several original Vroman negatives; to Dr. Ernest Bruch who so generously checked library and business records in Rockford, Illinois; and to Mr. Bill Murphy who first brought to my attention the excellence of the negatives.

Beyond that I owe thanks to Mr. William Webb who has so carefully and faithfully worked to reproduce the original quality of the negatives; and to Mr. Robert Weinstein whose enthusiasm and encouragement gave me the incentive to carry this project to a conclusion.

RUTH I. MAHOOD

TABLE OF CONTENTS

LIST OF PLATES

1899

ADAM CLARK VROMAN

by BEAUMONT NEWHALL

DAM CLARK VROMAN railroad man, book collector, bookseller, amateur archaeologist, and photographer, linked two great periods of Western photography. He was one of a small number of amateurs who continued the tradition of field photography begun in the 1860's by Timothy H. O'Sullivan, J. K. Hillers, and William Henry Jackson. And he anticipated the direct, precise, and sensitive styles of such twentieth-century photographers as Edward Weston and Ansel Adams.

His best work was done between 1895 and 1904 in Southern California, Arizona, and New Mexico—the area defined as the Southwest by his friend, Charles Fletcher Lummis, the New Englander who walked 3075 miles across the continent in 143 days to become city editor of the Los Angeles *Times*. Like Lummis, who was also an amateur photographer, Vroman's purpose was the documentation of the land, the Indians who lived on it, and the relics of the Spanish Colonial period. Others shared this purpose: George Wharton James, a writer, and Edward S. Curtis of Seattle who took as his lifetime dedication the photographic documentation of all the Indians in the United States.

This generation of field photographers faced problems which their predecessors had not known. The West was no longer wild. Tourists swarmed through the land, encouraged to travel by railroads, hotels, and Chambers of Commerce. Photography was no longer limited to those willing to master the difficult wet-plate process and to pack dark tents and processing equipment along with bulky tripod cameras and heavy glass plates. The invention of dry plates and roll film reduced photography to the pressing of a button. The Kodak, the Kamaret, the Photoret, the Bull's-Eye, the Hitormissit, the P. D. Q. ("Photography Done Quickly"), the Quad, the Alvista,

9

the Weno, the Premo, the Poco—these hand cameras and scores like them brought photography to all. Most tourists carried one, and in their greed to get pictures, they changed the life of the Indian by paying him to pose and making him so self-conscious that he even changed his ceremonies. By 1902 the Hopi Indians of the pueblo of Oraibi restricted photographers to a single area during the Snake Dance.

> This was an innovation [George Wharton James wrote in *Camera Craft*, November 1902]. Hitherto every man had chosen his own field, and moved to and fro wherever he liked—in front of his neighbor or someone else; kicking down another fellow's tripod and sticking his elbow in the next fellow's lens. Half a dozen or more Indian policemen led by the acting agent kept us in line, so we had to go ahead and make the best of it.

There was further photographic activity: motion picture producers were sending cameramen to film the dances. One of them appears in Vroman's photograph of the Snake Dance at Oraibi (page 97): Edison copyrighted in 1901 six films: "Indian Snake Dance Series in Moki Land."*

Thus, paradoxically, the very facility which had been brought to photography by technical improvements made photography in the Southwest all the more difficult—and all the more needful, for customs were already dying. Vroman succeeded in this difficult task. He avoided the sentimental, the contrived, and the obvious. He photographed simply, directly, and sympathetically.

How he became interested in photography remains as much a mystery as how he became a book collector—both somewhat surprising avocations for a railroad man. He worked for seventeen years for the Chicago, Burlington and Quincy Railroad at Rockford, Illinois, as operator, agent, train dispatcher, and ticket seller—a multiplication of duties which Lucius Beebe, the noted railroad historian, states was not unusual.

He was born in La Salle, Illinois, on April 15, 1856, a descendant of Hendrick Muse Vrooman, who came to America from Holland in 1664. When

---

*"Moki, Moqui, Hopi" are synonymous. Despite the plea of Lummis (see his *Mesa, Cañon, and Pueblo*, p. 495), the term "Hopi" is now universal.

Glasscock and Vroman store interior, Pasadena, 1895

The Glasscock and Vroman store, Pasadena, 1895

a relative sought information from him for a genealogy of the family, he had but little information to give her beyond the facts that his father was born in New York City and moved to Illinois about 1835. He explained, "Our knowledge is lacking as to much of his earlier life as I, leaving home at sixteen, did not become interested in our family matters until after his death."

In 1892 Vroman married Esther H. Griest. She suffered from tuberculosis, and in an effort to restore her health the couple moved from Rockford to Pasadena, California. The date of their arrival is not known, but the day after Christmas they stayed at the Echo Mountain House; the husband signed the register "Mr. and Mrs. A. C. Vrooman," using the ancestral spelling.

The move was in vain. Mrs. Vroman's condition worsened; it seemed unlikely that she could long survive; and a sad trip was made East across the continent to her home in Flora Dale, near Media, Pennsylvania. There, in September 1894, she died.

On his return to Pasadena, Vroman sold his collection of fine books to raise capital for establishing a bookstore with J. S. Glasscock, which they opened on November 14, 1894. He shortly acquired full title to the business, and bookselling remained his profession for the rest of his life. The store he founded still flourishes, and still enjoys a fine reputation.

As an amateur photographer, Vroman found California and the Southwest "the long-looked-for land of opportunities." He did not agree with his friend Lummis who, although an accomplished photographer, wrote in his *Land of Poco Tiempo:*

> New Mexico, like the dearest women, cannot be adequately photographed. One can reproduce the features, but not the expression—the landmarks, but not the wondrous light which is to the bare Southwest the soul that glorifies a plain face. . . . One cannot focus upon sunlight and silence.[1]

Vroman did precisely that. It would almost seem that he took Lummis's complaint as a challenge. He made his first trip to Hopi land, Arizona, in 1895; the magnificent landscape "Twin Buttes" (page 75), serves as an over-

[1]Charles Fletcher Lummis, *The Land of Poco Tiempo* (New York: Charles Scribner's Sons, 1893), p. 9.

ture. He visted Tewa and at Walpi made photographs which Lummis published in his magazine, *The Land of Sunshine*, to illustrate an article, "The Moqui Snake Dance," by H. N. Rust.

The Indians became his friends. He never forgot to bring them the promised prints, and they looked forward to his return year after year. His photographs of them are portraits of personalities, not records of aborigines. They are individuals, not characteristic types. And they look straight at the eye of the camera, unflinching, unafraid, though they were brought up by their fathers to believe, as Lummis wrote, "that the photograph was taken not only of them, but *from* them; and that, with enough prints, they would waste away to nothingness."[2]

Vroman tells, in a series of articles in *Photo Era* magazine in 1901 how he succeeded in winning the confidence of the Indian.

> If you are a little patient, and do not try to hurry matters you will have but little trouble in getting what you want. The Indian must always have plenty of time to think over anything he has to do, and you cannot rush him a particle; sit down with him, show him the camera inside and out, stand on your head (on the ground-glass) for him, or anything you want him to do, and he will do the same for you. One trouble is a lack of background. If you take the time to improvise one, the subject may change his mind and your time is wasted.[3]

What a contrast to the casual photographer in search of "picturesque bits"! George Wharton James photographed in the same pueblos which Vroman visited. In an article "Photographing Indian Babies" in *Camera Craft* he reproduces a picture he took of a Hopi Indian boy carrying an infant in his arms. The hair falls over his face like a sheep dog's; the baby writhes in impatience; a grotesque shadow of the pair cuts diagonally across the picture. And this is what James wrote:

> Where else in all the world could such a funny picture be made. Look at the "catch-as-catch-can" fashion of the boy baby carrier.

[2]Charles Fletcher Lummis, *Mesa, Cañon and Pueblo* (New York: The Century Co., 1925), p. ix.

[3]*Photo Era*, VI (1901), 269-70.

See the arms of the baby, and the way her little legs are tossed hither and thither, and the peculiar wiggle of the toes, as shown clearly by the shadow of the turned-up foot. Then look at the boy's lips. Even though his eyes cannot be seen the lips have such a distinctly ugly pout that you can feel the burning indignation and anger of the eyes (at being thus held up) shooting through the matted hair which falls over his forehead. His shirt might have been a little longer, or shorter, either would have done, and the shadow just as it is. Altogether it is a picture to be grateful for; for it gives fun and enjoyment, and what more does any artist, amateur or professional, want?[4]

Yet James professed sympathy for the Indians, and the need of recording their fast-vanishing customs. Many of his photographs, particularly of the Snake Dance at Oraibi, rival those of Vroman in both technical and documentary quality.

Vroman had little to say about technique in his *Photo Era* articles. The negatives of his which exist are almost all 6½-by-8½-inch glass plates. He exposed them in a view camera. He must have experienced the same problems that James, who used the same size camera, faced.

Generally speaking, climactic and actinic conditions are perfect in Arizona and New Mexico for instantaneous out-door work. But it is a hard country on cameras. Miles and miles have to be made over rough roads, where fine sand sifts into everything, so that shutters and catches, etc., do not work, and one often has to fall back upon the old-time cap. Many of my exposures are cap exposures perforce.[5]

Vroman had an extraordinary appreciation of the quality of the light of the Southwest, described by Lummis as "a photographic light to be matched in no other civilized country. It glows upon the desert of Egypt, or the pampas of the Andes, across the llanos of New Mexico. . . . The most careless and untrained eye realizes something of this effect; but the pho-

[4]*Camera Craft*, VI (1902), 58-59.
[5]*Ibid.*, p. 58.

14

A. C. Vroman, 1893

A. C. Vroman, 1897

A. C. Vroman, 1897

Esther Griest Vroman, 1894

tographer at once discovers that sunlight here is, in technical results, as different a thing from sunlight in New York or England as the sky from a second-hand tin pan. It gives him cameos of definition, wonders of detail, and a real revelation in antitheses of light and shade, vigorous without being violent. . . . It is, in fact, the sky of Spanish America; and somehow, wherever that bends there are certain picturesquenesses which seem to belong to it."[6]

Clouds—"such beautiful clouds as only the light clear air of the southwest can produce"[7]—particularly appealed to Vroman, and to record them he used Cramer's Isochromatic plates. These plates, forerunners of modern orthochromatic films, were more sensitive to green and yellow, and less sensitive to blue, than ordinary dry plates. They are listed in the 1892 catalogue of E. & H. T. Anthony, the New York photographic stockhouse, as a new product—though other brands of similar characteristics had been available since 1883.* The increased color sensitivity of the "Iso" plates enabled Vroman to darken the sky by putting a yellow screen, or "ray filter" over the lens.

He made brilliant use of this new material to capture the vast landscapes of the Southwest; his best plates presage the work that Paul Strand and Ansel Adams were to do under the same skies, some thirty years later.

He printed his negatives on platinum paper. This beautiful material, no longer made, gave images of great delicacy, with a long range of tones in the middle greys. The paper was put in contact with the negative in a frame, and exposed to daylight. Enlargements could be obtained only by first producing an enlarged negative, a process so laborious that it was little used.

The reproductions in this book are not from Vroman's original platinotypes, however, but from prints made for the purpose by William Webb on modern paper. To the making of them Webb has brought the experience of a skilled and sensitive photographer aware and appreciative of the tra-

[6]*Land of Sunshine*, II (1895), 28-29.

[7]*Photo Era*, VI (1901), 230.

*On the history of the color sensitivity of photographic emulsions, see John Carbutt, "The Polychrome Plate," *Wilson's Photographic Mag.*, XL (1903), 171-73, and C. E. K. Mees, *The Theory of the Photographic Process* (rev. ed.; New York: the Macmillan Company, 1954), pp. 354-57. Cramer's Isochromatic plates were not sensitive to red rays and hence not truly panchromatic.

dition of "straight photography" of the nineteenth-century pioneers and of those twentieth-century photographers who formed an esthetic based upon the simplest and most direct use of the camera. The rediscovery of the esthetic value of Vroman's work is due to Webb's perception and interpretation.

Although Vroman was an Eastman Kodak Company dealer, and derived a substantial part of his bookstore profits from the agency, he preferred the traditional view camera for most of his work. He notes in his *Photo Era* article that Indian children scamper "as you turn on the Kodak," and he can be seen holding small folding cameras, presumably for roll film, in the group picture at San Juan Capistrano (page 63) and in the self-portrait at the Cañon de Chelly in 1904 (page 120). But the view camera was his love. It cost him much effort. Dr. Frederick Webb Hodge, who led the Bureau of American Ethnology expeditions to the pueblos in 1897 recollected that "Vroman's equipment of camera, tripod, negatives, and supplies, weighed at least fifty pounds, all of which he carried himself. In fact, he wouldn't let anyone touch it. I actually believe he wrapped it up with him in his bedroll every night!"[8]

His choice was logical. Only with the larger camera could he record the richness of detail needed to give his photographs value as documents. He liked his photographs sharp, precisely focused, fully realized.

One must never, in judging Vroman's work, overlook its purpose: he was a documentary photographer. Every photograph he took primarily for its informational value. He was gifted with a remarkable vision, and often endowed his pictures with qualities that go beyond the record of a moment or a place. Although he was an amateur, he was employed as official photographer on two expeditions of the Bureau of American Ethnology. In 1897 he accompanied Dr. Hodge on a climb to the top of Katzimo, the Enchanted Mesa, and secured photographic evidence of the truth of the Indian legend that once the pueblo of Acoma was located there. The story of the ascent, and of the archaeological controversy that led to its undertaking, is best told by Vroman himself in the *Photo Era* article which is reprinted on pages 31-34.

Every phase of Southwest history interested Vroman. He shared with

[8]Lawrence Clark Powell, "Photographer of the Southwest," *Westways*, L. No. 8, Part 1 (Aug., 1958), 13.

Charles F. Lummis a deep concern for Spanish America. He made a special study of the background of Helen Hunt Jackson's *Ramona* which, together with twenty-four of his photographs was published as an introduction to an edition of the novel by Little, Brown and Co. in 1915. The photographs show the settings of the story: the ranchos of Camulos and Guajome, the missions of Santa Barbara, San Gabriel, and San Luis Rey. His essay is a photographer's appreciation of Mrs. Jackson's power of observation, for he was able to duplicate to the most minute detail many of the scenes she described. It seems that Mrs. Jackson began research for her novel—which she undertook as a protest against the mistreatment of Indians—as a guest of Señora Coutts at the ranch of Guajome, 70 miles south of Los Angeles. Friction developed between guest and hostess, and Mrs. Jackson was asked to leave the ranch and was "forbidden the use of it as the home of her heroine."

In despair Mrs. Jackson turned to a friend, in the hope that the matters could be arranged so that she could return to Guajome. Instead the friend took her to Camulos, a similar ranch. She spent only two hours there —yet her descriptions Vroman found exact. The only mistake he noted was that she counted five steps leading up the verandah at Camulos; his photograph shows eight. But Mrs. Jackson described exactly the bench, the Indian jar, and the yucca beside the entrance.

Apparently the last trip Vroman made to the Southwest was in 1904, when he visited the Cañon de Chelly and went back to see his Hopi friends. Edward S. Curtis was in the same area. The styles of these two photographers are vividly defined in the photographs which each took of the same great rock wall of the Cañon de Chelly. Both included human figures to emphasize its thousand-foot height. Vroman chose to include the wagon which had brought him and his companions to the scene. He chose a time of day when the light shone full upon the great rock wall. Curtis shows mounted Indians walking their horses in single file into the setting sun, which grazes the cliff, throwing most of it in shadow. The work of Curtis was already well known. Arnold Genthe, reviewing the First San Francisco Photographic Salon of 1901, noted that "E. S. Curtis' Indian studies occupy quite a place by themselves. They are of immense ethnological value as an excellent record of a dying race, and most of them are really picturesque, showing good composition and interesting light effects."[9] In 1905 Curtis held an exhibition in the Waldorf Astoria in New York of a collection of several hundred photographs. John A. Tennant, in his magazine *Photo-Miniature*, wrote:

> It is not difficult to appreciate the immense value and importance of this work to the ethnologist, the historian, and the artist. . . . Viewed as a whole, the undertaking is the most remarkable artistic and historical work thus far attempted by photography in America. It has been enthusiastically endorsed by President Roosevelt, the Bureau of American Ethnology at Washington, and other eminent authorities in this special field.[10]

With the backing of John Pierpont Morgan, a series of handsome volumes and portfolios of fine reproductions of Curtis's photographs began to appear, until forty were published.

Until the present volume, Vroman's photographs were scarcely known. The reproductions of the few which were published in *Photo Era*, in *The Land of Sunshine*, and in books, are so poor that the quality of the image is lost. He kept apart from organized amateur photography. We do not find his name in the amateur photographic periodicals as a camera club member or exhibitor. In 1898 he wrote to the California Club in San Francisco for advice on organizing a camera club in Southern California. They sent him their constitution and bylaws and he formed what the "Auld Lang Syne" column of the *Pasadena Star News* in 1952 described as "a small group of congenial souls who met in Mr. Vroman's library above his bookstore at 60 East Colorado St., Pasadena." Page 63 shows "The Club" on a field trip to San Juan Capistrano Mission; all five members present have cameras. But when the Los Angeles Camera Club was founded in December 1900, Vroman's name does not appear in the membership list.

This is not surprising, for the West Coast camera clubs were only pale imitations of the Camera Club in New York which, under the dynamic influence of Alfred Stieglitz, was a spearhead of amateur photography until

[9]*Camera Craft*, II (Feb. 1901), 310.
[10]*Photo-Miniature*, VI, No. 72 (Sep., 1905), 663.

the formation of the Photo-Secession in 1902. To judge from the reproductions in *Camera Craft*, the photographs of the California pictorialists were weak imitations of the styles of the Photo-Secession, lacking in taste, technique, and conviction.

In 1909 Vroman went to Japan and the Far East to collect Oriental art. His collection of Netsuke carvings was acquired by the Metropolitan Museum of Art. On the trip he photographed with a small camera. But the negatives have no longer the quality which distinguishes the earlier work.

He died, aged sixty, from pernicious anemia in Altadena, California, on July 24, 1916.

He was mourned by the community.

> Piercing through Mr. Vroman's characteristics and tendencies and achievements, there shines out with steady brightness qualities that most endeared him to those who knew him well—his sense of justice, his solicitous consideration for the rights of others, his sympathetic affection for friends and associates, his helpful interest in those whom help might benefit. . . . He exemplified the conviction that life is worth living.[11]

His photographic work was forgotten, even though he left sixteen volumes of platinotypes to the Pasadena Public Library. The 2400 negatives which were sold by the estate to the Los Angeles County Board of Education were promptly filed by the Audio-Visual Department and forgotten until recently, when they were rediscovered through the curiosity of Lawrence Clark Powell, Dean of the School of Library Service, University of California, Los Angeles, and Ruth Mahood, the County Museum's Curator of History.

This is the first book publication of the photographic work of Adam Clark Vroman. Most of the photographs have never been reproduced in any form. They reveal him as a sensitive, gifted photographer, whose work of unquestioned documentary value is a proud heritage in the history of American photography.

[11]John Steven McGroarty, *History of Los Angeles County* (New York: American Historical Society, 1923), pp. 413-14.

20

DISCOVERY OF THE LOST VROMAN PLATES

by RUTH I. MAHOOD

RECORDING OF HISTORICAL EVIDENCE has, since the middle of the nineteenth century, been the contribution of some photographers. Such a photographer was Adam Clark Vroman.

The discovery of his important work, lost in obscurity for many years, is the "saga" of the some twenty-four hundred 6½-by-8½-inch glass photographic negatives now in the collection of the Division of History at the Los Angeles County Museum. They were first brought to my attention in 1957. It was Lawrence Clark Powell of the University of California, Los Angeles, Library who started the search that uncovered these plates. Dr. Powell was asked to write a brochure in honor of the grand opening of the new Vroman's at 695 East Colorado Street, Pasadena, California, on October 8, 1953, an establishment which opened its doors for business in 1894, sixty-seven years ago. Dr. Powell, who at one time had been a delivery boy for Vroman's, believed that still in existence must be the glass plates of the many pictures Mr. Vroman had taken in his career as a photographer. With the help of the late Dr. F. W. Hodge, anthropologist and former Director of the Southwest Museum, he located them in the possession of the Los Angeles County Schools. They were stored in metal file cabinets and appeared to be in fairly good shape. No one had realized the importance of these plates and they had been stored in ground floor storerooms. In February 1954 these cabinets were removed to the Los Angeles County Museum.

To trace the history of these plates, a former employee of the Los Angeles County Schools was consulted. She stated that they were purchased from the A. C. Vroman estate sometime before 1920 for use by the Audio-

Visual Division. There is evidence they were used by the County Schools because there is a nearly complete set of 5-by-7-inch positive film transparencies with the collection. This is fortunate because some of the plates have been cracked and some broken beyond use in the years since they were stored. The exact date of storage by the County Schools is not known.

Actual research on the negatives began one day in January 1957, when I received a call from the Business Manager of the County Schools. He said, "I have *some more* of those glass negatives. What do you want me to do with them?" At the time I hadn't the slightest idea what he was talking about. But I did have sense enough to say, after a short hesitation, "Do what you did with the others." It was the right answer because he said, "Fine," and hung up.

A few days later our shipping clerk called me to say there were a couple of boxes of old broken glass down there for me. Realizing it must be the negatives I had them sent up to my office.

Curiosity prompted investigation. The plates were in brown envelopes, numbered and labeled in Mr. Vroman's own inimitable copperplate handwriting. This might be a reminder to all people who collect and photograph to identify the location, persons, date, and any other pertinent information which would save much work in identification later. The first negative was one of Mission San Luis Rey. I held it up to the light and as the image came through sharp and clear I realized that these plates were something special. Until this time, A. C. Vroman was known to me only as the founder of a bookstore in Pasadena, California.

There were only about two hundred and fifty negatives. Where were the others? I began a search which ended in the County Museum Registrar's office with the hope that she might know about them. She looked in her files and found an inventory. When the first plates came to the Museum, a faded and hardly legible inventory came with them. She had deciphered that inventory and had made several typed copies. She told me the plates were stored in the basement of the Education Division.

The collection has been checked thoroughly, completely catalogued, and re-enveloped so the plates are easily accessible when they are wanted. In making the survey it was found that a number of the plates were badly cracked and that some of them were broken beyond repair. This probably occurred during the various moves. If there was any possibility of saving the negative it was carefully pieced together and stored. Some, which were really ground glass, had to be discarded. All possible care was taken to preserve as many as possible.

To do a thorough inventory of these plates required the work of many months. As has been stated, there was an inventory of sorts and each negative had been numbered. The inventory carried two separate numbers for each plate; a "V.E.D." (Visual Education Department) number presumably was that assigned by the Los Angeles County Schools to facilitate their use. This list ran numerically but did not coincide with another listed as "Vroman Number," presumably A. C. Vroman's own number. No definite conclusion has been reached regarding the relationship. The Museum uses the "V.E.D." for its accession numbers.

The Los Angeles County Museum had a first Vroman exhibition in the summer of 1958, showing about eighty-five sepia reproductions chosen from the negatives of the missions and of Yosemite—only eighty-five of the some twenty-four hundred in the collection. The many comments by the public who saw them and the requests for prints only added to my first impression of their importance. In September 1960, a permanent Vroman gallery was opened. From time to time the prints in this gallery will be changed to afford the public the opportunity of enjoying the majority of the large number of photographs and the variety of subject matter the collection contains.

Vroman was a skilled photographer as the plates have indicated. It was through his interest in photography that he was able to leave this representative collection of a record of the California Missions before restoration, the splendors of Yosemite, the scenic beauty of Pasadena and surrounding areas, a record of a trip to the East, and finally, a complete record of several expeditions to the pueblos of New Mexico and Arizona, led by the late Frederick Webb Hodge.

It was between 1895 and 1905 that he visited all the California missions and made his photographic record. He took them from every angle, interiors and exteriors. Only a love for his work and its subjects could have produced this monument to his labors. He truly was a perfectionist! Realize that for transportation he had to depend on the horse and buggy.

To cite Mr. Vroman while in New Mexico on an expedition, "After a day's drive in a lumber wagon, or at best, a buckboard, sand makes a first-rate bed."

A trip to Yosemite produced a series of scenes about the turn of the century. It is interesting to compare recent pictures with those taken by Mr. Vroman.

In 1897, the late Dr. F. W. Hodge led a Bureau of Ethnology expedition to the pueblos. Dr. Hodge was particularly interested in photographs of the ascent of the Enchanted Mesa (Mesa Encantada). There was a dispute at the time between Professor William Libbey of Princeton College and Dr. Hodge as to whether it had been inhabited by Indians. Libbey had earlier visited the "cairn" or monument on top of the mesa and had decided that it was "the results of erosion." After the Hodge party had made the ascent, Libbey confessed that the famous "cairn" was built with hands. He had seen Mr. Vroman's, in the words of C. F. Lummis, "deadly photograph." In his own inimitable way Lummis also wrote in *Land of Sunshine*, October 1897, in an article, "The Disenchanted Libbey," that "Mr. Vroman's beautiful photographs carry startling proof of the unparalleled innocence of Professor Libbey." It was the actual ascent of the Enchanted Mesa by the Hodge party, and the photographs taken by Mr. Vroman, that made it possible to prove previous habitation on the Mesa.

An interesting sidelight concerning the expedition was told by Dr. Hodge. It seems that Mr. Vroman completely lacked a sense of direction. "He used to set up his tripod in the midst of juniper and piñon stands, walk away a short distance to see if he could get a better shot of Acoma, for example, and then become lost. I was always having to find his tripod for him!"

It was again in 1899 that Mr. Vroman accompanied, as photographer, an expedition of the Bureau of American Ethnology into the Southwest to examine the Indian pueblos and ruins of ancient cliff dwellers. Dr. Hodge again was in charge of the party which included Dr. Elliot Coues, George Parker Winship, William H. Guilford, and Albert J. Bird. The Santa Fe *New Mexican* of July 28, 1899 states, "The main object of the party is to visit as many pueblos of New Mexico as possible and to obtain a large and complete series of photographs."

The scientists traveled 650 miles in their wagon, camping every night, and visited all the pueblos from Taos to Zuñi, besides a lot of unknown ruins. The Pasadena *Daily Evening Star* of August 29, 1899 states, "They found the ruins of the Cibolitta Valley and of the Santa Clara canyon the most interesting, being the best preserved. Mr. Vroman is wearing a dark brown complexion and looks a little thin but says he is now feeling well and brought his appetite home with him."

In connection with the expedition, Mr. Vroman wrote a series of articles for *Photo Era* which appeared between January and October 1901. In addition to the one on "The Enchanted Mesa," there were "The Moki Pueblos," "The Moki Snake Dance," "The Petrified Forest of Arizona," "The Pueblos of Zuñi," and "Photography in the Great Southwest." Here is Mr. Vroman's picture of the Pueblo Indian:

"We've been educated from time immemorial that the Indian is a devil incarnate, only waiting to cut your throat and scalp you! Not so. After portions of five summers spent among the Pueblos, I am willing to vouch for fair treatment at their hands, and in fact, he will go more than his share of the way every time to do right. Have no fear of the Indian; it is the bad white man that you should be watchful of in this country."

And again, "The Indian is a sympathetic fellow, appreciates kindness and never forgets a friend. I have no liking for the man who has been among the Indians and says that 'all good Indians are dead Indians,' and for those who have never been among them, and hold such opinions, a summer's outing among the Pueblos will, I am sure, bring on a change of heart. I speak only for the Pueblo Indian, as I know nothing of the Plains Indian, but have no fear but he will average with us in honor and truthfulness."

Because of his deep love for his adopted Southwest, for the missions, and for all that pertains to the romantic period of the state's history, he was able by artistic photography, by printed words, and by lectures and conversation to illuminate the annals of past times in California.

A short time before his death, he did an interesting and enlightening introduction to a late edition of *Ramona* in which he told of his personal observation at the scenes where the story is laid and threw entertaining sidelights on the author and her different characters. This also appeared in book form titled, *The Genesis of the Story of Ramona*. The introduction states that "To unravel the tangle is the aim of the article, and if possible, work out the genesis of the story in such a manner as seems necessary for the better understanding of the book." With this thought, the writer made a careful search for any information on the subject available and obtainable.

In the book, he explains some of the apparent inconsistencies as to the location of some of the scenes. The little book is thoroughly illustrated by his delightful photographs of scenes of the locale of the book.

He was an art collector. Many of his treasures were found among the Indians. He was particularly proud of the Navajo blankets: " . . . one of those marvelously beautiful ones that are so much sought after just at this time, and which to me are so much more interesting and beautiful than any Persian or Turkish rugs, and why should we not value the handiwork of our native Indians as much as a foreign purchase? It will be but a few years before an Indian blanket will be as rare as a buffalo skin is today." There were also Kachina dolls in the collection that he turned over to the Southwest Museum.

He sought to create interest in the Southwest by presenting to the people of Pasadena his pictorial record. He gave the Pasadena Public Library sixteen green morocco-bound and gold-tooled albums of mounted photographs of California and the Southwest, taken in the late 1880's and through the early 1900's. He also bequeathed to the library a collection of books on the Southwest, together with $10,000 to augment the collection.

During all this time, the bookstore at 60 East Colorado Street prospered. The inventory increased each year until, in 1916, it reached 30,000 titles. Before his death, he made arrangements for his employees to acquire interest in the substantial business that they had. To aid his employees in purchasing stock, he included them in his will, bequeathing to each $100 for each year of service in the store.

Mr. Vroman died of pernicious anemia on July 24, 1916 at the Altadena home of a business associate, George F. Howell. He was 60 years old. His estate was valued at $100,000 and was distributed among friends and relatives in a variety of bequests. At his request, his ashes were scattered over his wife's grave in the Friends Cemetery in Flora Dale, Pennsylvania.

PRINTING THE VROMAN NEGATIVES

by WILLIAM WEBB

T HE SCARCITY OF ORIGINAL VROMAN PRINTS, which might have formed the basis for the reproductions in this book, has compelled the publisher to order a complete set of new prints made from the original Vroman negatives. With an occasional exception, all the reproductions in this volume began with these new prints.

In order to recreate, as much as possible, the intent of each image as it was probably conceived by Mr. Vroman, a close study of the surviving Vroman prints was made. The primary source of these is the collection of platinotypes in the Pasadena Public Library. However, because of the self-compensating quality of this printing medium there is a softness and length of scale in these prints which belies the fact that some of the negatives from which they were produced had density ranges in excess of 3.00. Also, the means by which the platinotypes were exposed—direct sunlight—precluded any elaborate local control through dodging, burning, etc.

Fortunately, a handful of original chloride prints in the collection of Mr. Vroman's niece, Mrs. Oscar Wiedmann of Shafter, California, was available for study. These prints, which were probably made towards the end of Mr. Vroman's life, indicate an uncommon sensitivity to print quality. Each print was a beautiful example of a full scale of values organized for maximum emotional impact, equal to the finest in modern printing. From these one could derive a clear direction as to how to proceed with the making of the new prints.

There is reason to believe, incidentally, that Vroman did not practice enlarging beyond the making of an occasional print. The tonal degradation inherent in the projection techniques of the day doubtless discouraged serious efforts in this direction.

The technical difficulties encountered in making the contemporary prints arose out of the need for adapting modern printing papers to negatives scaled primarily for printing-out papers. A negative that would yield a brilliant platinotype would often be unprintable on grade "0" contact paper. In extreme conditions this problem was met by making a duplicate negative from a transparent interpositive.

More serious was the large number of negatives which had suffered deterioration in storage. Coping with silver stains, developer stains, or faded images involved an assortment of techniques ranging from making duplicate negatives to wholesale restorative treatments on the original.

Vroman, not unlike photographers before and since his time, was the occasional victim of the exposure and/or processing disaster. Given to experimentation, he seems to have tried about every new emulsion as it came along. Equipped with a new panchromatic emulsion on his 1904 trip to Cañon de Chelly, he consistently underexposed and overdeveloped every plate. This calamity was compounded by the fact that Vroman was at top form in visualization on this trip, and apart from the technical blemishes, the de Chelly series represents some of his most eloquent images.

Generally speaking, most of the negatives were printed on standard chloride papers, primarily grades "0" and "1." The prints were developed in Amidol and given a slight selenium tone. Benzotriazole was included in the Amidol formula to preserve the clearest whites possible. Since reproduction was to be by offset lithography, prints were made to full scale to take advantage of the one-to-one tonal rendition of which lithography is capable.

Some of the prints were made on "sun-proof" paper when the scale of the original negatives was so long as to be unprintable on chloride papers. In such cases exposures were heavy to render a somewhat heavier than normal image. The print was then washed in plain water, gold-toned, and fixed in plain hypo. Fidelity to some of the original Vroman "solio" prints was remarkable.

Cropping of the prints was conservative, based upon the cropping of the platinotypes in the Pasadena Library collection. In the majority of cases Vroman composed to the edge of his plates. Some liberties were taken here and there to eliminate unsightly blotches and evidences of deterioration either by cropping them out or by spotting and retouching. This, however, has been kept at a minimum.

Vroman appears to have left no technical data which might have been of interest to a modern photographer.

NOTES ON THE ILLUSTRATIONS

IT IS NOT POSSIBLE TO COMPRESS into the brief compass of this book anything more than a smattering of the total photographic output left by Adam Clark Vroman. A broad survey, illustrated with selected examples, must suffice to indicate the stature of the man and his work.

This section begins with an article about the ascent of the Enchanted Mesa in New Mexico. The story was written by Mr. Vroman for *Photo-Era* of October 1901. Its inclusion here is to place in perspective the involvement of the man in his beloved Southwest, as well as to illustrate one of the ways that he put his photographs to use. This article is not presented in facsimile, but typographic design and placement of the illustrations suggest the appearance of the original.

The balance of the pictures is sufficiently self-explanatory, though some comment on the pictures of the Indians is in order. Vroman photographed in a period when the trust by the Indian of the white man had not been so shamefully betrayed as it has become in our time. There were no particular restrictions, then, about photographing the Hopi Snake Dance. In later times commercialization and ridicule by the white man of their ceremonies have provoked most Indians to stringent prohibitions against photography. It is no longer possible to win the kind of coöperation so freely given to Vroman, which enabled him to record not only the ceremonies, but almost all aspects of Indian life of the period. The elegant environmental portraits which grace this part of the book are testimony to the trust which Vroman enjoyed from a people by nature jealous of their privacy.

The pictures of Nampeyo will be particularly appreciated by those acquainted with the history of Hopi pottery. This extraordinary potter participated in the excavations of Sikyatki and collected many of the potsherds uncovered. From the designs of these relics she recreated and revived the ancient, but virtually lost, art of pottery-making among the Hopi. Her wares became very popular among the whites and their sale went far to bolster the sagging Hopi economy as well as restore dignity to a people who were already beginning to lose touch with a proud past. Today Nampeyo is remembered by all Hopis with an affection accorded few others.

Mesa Encantada, the mesa from the east

KATZIMO, THE ENCHANTED MESA

BY A. C. VROMAN

PROBABLY not more than a few hundred people could be found prior to 1897, who had ever heard of the "Mesa Encantada" or Enchanted Mesa, as it is generally known, or as the natives call it, "Katzimo." Yet for more than three hundred and fifty years, it has been known as the "inaccessible rock," from the chroniclers of Coronado's time, to the Government Survey Reports following the transfer of the country from Mexico to the United States, and other accounts. Bandelier, than whom there is no greater authority on the southwest, says, speaking of the mesa, "a towering isolated mesa with vertical sides several hundred feet in height, utterly inaccessible." (See papers Arch. Institute of America, Am. Series, Vol. IV, page 313.)

Some twelve or fourteen years ago, Mr. Charles F. Lummis, in St. Nicholas, published an article in which he gave the first account of the Acoma tradition.—That, at one time ages ago, the pueblo of Acoma was located on the top of Katzimo, and that one day when all who were able to work were in the fields gathering the harvest, there came a great storm, or cloudburst, and the quantities of water undermined the great ladder rock, the only means of access to the top. It came down with a mighty crash, leaving two old women, a boy named Achite, and his mother who had been left in charge of the pueblo, on top of the mesa unable to reach the valley. For days afterward, the natives circled around the great rock, but it was never to be their home again. No ladder could be built up so perpendicular a wall. Councils were held and sacrifices were made, but still no way of reaching the top presented itself, and at last it was decided to build a new Acoma,

the same we know today, three miles to the southwest on a mesa some one hundred and fifty feet lower, yet not unlike Katzimo. Here Coronado in 1540 found the pueblo of Acoma, much as we see it today.

Mr. Lummis gives the tradition as it was told to him by one of the old principales of the pueblo, and verified by others until convinced of its authenticity.

Katzimo is fifteen miles southwest from Laguna, a station on the Santa Fe route sixty-five miles west of Albuquerque, New Mexico, and is best reached from Laguna, where accommodations and conveyance can be had. Cubero station would be some six miles nearer but no conveyance can be had from this point, and besides the pueblo of

Mesa Encantada, beginning the ascent

Laguna is well worth seeing. The mesa can be seen for an instant from the car window at two points, on close watch, between other mesas and buttes just before the train reaches Cubero station.

Katzimo itself is a huge rock rising abruptly from the valley and towering four hundred and thirty-one feet with almost perpendicular walls on all sides, except at one point near the south end where a crevasse has been washed out, perhaps one hundred feet across, leaving a great mass of talus reaching halfway to the top of the mesa. Approaching from Laguna you get a first sight from a point nearly five miles away and you do not realize its immensity until you see how long it has taken you to drive by it. You think, a few minutes and it will be out of reach of the camera. But after half an hour you think it is like trouble, always with you.

Standing as it does, an island as it were in the valley, four hundred and thirty-one feet sheer up without a break, it was an ideal place for a pueblo and must have been the envy of the other pueblos, and the desire of many an exploring party to reach the summit. But the three hundred and fifty year record of "inaccessible," discouraged all until September, 1895. Then Mr. F. W. Hodge of the Bureau of American Ethnology while searching the talus for potsherds, climbed up the crevasse above mentioned, to a point some three hundred feet above the valley, and would then have reached the top; but being alone, having no rope, and realizing the difficulty in getting down from such a place, he gave it up for the time, but determined the next summer to come prepared, and make the ascent. On reaching Washington he had constructed six ladders, six feet each in length, of light material and built so that one section could be slipped in from below and fastened, and then another and another added, and so on until all were in use.

Mr. Hodge was detained in Washington the following year however, and did not ship his outfit until 1897, when after witnessing the Snake Dance at Walpi, in August, he would be ready for the mesa.

Mr. Hodge was anticipated, however, four or five weeks by Professor Libby of Princeton University, who threw a line over the south point of the mesa by the aid of a small cannon, and after four days hauling of rope

Mesa Encantada, ascending the prehistoric trail.

at last got over a cable strong enough to support the weight of a man. This was securely fastened at each end and a block and pulley attached where the cable rested on the top of the mesa. Through this another rope ran to the foot of the mesa, and Professor Libby and an assistant were hauled to the top.

The line had been thrown over the south end where it was very narrow and cut off from the larger part by a narrow crevasse some fifty feet deep and four feet across the top. In order to cross this he was obliged to send to Acoma, three miles distant for a ladder; the four feet might have been jumped easily, but with only a four-foot landing place and the chance of a three or four hundred-foot fall the risk was too great. By the time the ladder reached him it was so late that only a hurried inspection was made, and he returned to the valley.

Mesa Encantada, going up—the last pitch

Evidently the Professor did not realize the great importance of a thorough search of the summit for evidence of a previous occupation, as in his published report he says there was no evidence that the foot of man had ever trod the top of the mesa before his own. This did not deter Mr. Hodge from carrying out his own ideas as to reaching the top, nor his faith in Indian tradition and lore.

Arriving at the foot of the mesa about noon, Sept. 3d, in company with Maj. Pratt, a civil engineer from Laguna, myself and one other, we pitched camp and at fifteen minutes after one o'clock, each of us took what he could carry of ladders and rope, photographic outfit, etc. and started.

The first two hundred and twenty feet of rise to the top of the talus was comparatively easy, rather up hill and full of large stones, loose rock, etc., but not difficult. Then came a twelve foot wall which with the ladders was scaled without trouble, and which was called the first landing, or shelf. Then a rise of about fifty feet on a gradually sloping rock in a distance of perhaps two hundred feet, not difficult, but slippery. By stringing a rope to pull against one could steady himself and walk right up. We were not right in the crevasse, and hauled all the ladders, rope, and other outfit up to this point, and here real climbing commenced. Splicing three of the ladders together for a perpendicular wall of twenty feet we found an inclined smooth surfaced rock which necessitated finger and toe hold, until a rope was stretched for another twenty-five feet, and the third landing was reached. It now began to look a long way down (some two hundred and seventy-five feet) but by fastening a rope to a large boulder and dropping the other end down to the talus we had an alpine line to this point. When the ladders, etc., were hauled to this shelf, which was only four feet wide and possibly twenty long in a semi-circle, it left but little working space, and here Mr. Hodge's idea of constructing the ladder came in good play. On this little shelf, two hundred and seventy-five feet above the valley a long ladder could not have been raised, but by raising one six foot section up and sliding another in, and raising the two and adding another and another until all were in place, giving thirty-six feet of ladder, the next shelf was reached. Not however without some fear and trembling, for the next shelf was a more than perpendicular; overhanging nearly a foot, thus giving but three foot slant to the thirty-six foot ladder, and the first man to go up hugged that ladder about as close as a man could, while the other three held it from going over backward. This was the only really dangerous part of the ascent. After the first one was up, he held the top of the ladder until the next one came up with a rope, when it was tied and there was no further trouble.

The rest of the climb to the summit was almost as easy as some stairways, especially so after a rope had been strung along the face of the rock; and at half past three the entire party stood on the top of Katzimo, "the inaccessible" for more than three hundred years, with a feeling of satisfaction in accomplishing for the first time the real scaling of the Mesa Encantada.

It was soon decided to spend the night on the summit and after the two Indian drivers attached the camp outfit to the rope at the top of the talus, it was hauled up, and that evening the natives of Acoma must have been startled when on top of Katzimo they saw a great fire made from the dead cedars which covered the summit. For once indeed the place might well be called "the enchanted," and early the next morning a delegation of Acoma Indians appeared to investigate the cause, using the ropes that had been run along the trail. At first they appeared very much displeased but soon joined in the search for evidence of a previous occupation.

Mr. Hodge had picked up an arrow point, several pieces of broken pottery and two or three pieces of shell ornament during the evening, and the next morning found several other articles. One of the Indians picked up a broken stone hatchet, arrow points, etc. There was however, no sign of a pueblo ruin in the way of buildings.

There is, or has been, quite a growth of trees on the mesa; but nearly all were dead, probably from lack of soil, which the storms of wind and water destroy, for the wind is as great a reducing agent as the water in the desert country. This is quite significant, for if at one time there was soil enough to mature trees, twelve or more inches in diameter and they are now dying for lack of it, the same cause would remove all traces of adobe buildings, in the centuries that have passed since tradition says the Indians left Katzimo.

Maj. Pratt made a survey and map of the summit: extreme length two thousand seven hundred feet, and four to six hundred feet in width, the north end being the wider; the south end running down to a point; very irregular in outline, with a drop of eight to twenty-five feet from center to edge and especially at the south end, where great crevasses three to seven feet deep, have been cut away by the storms of years.

The night was quite chilly and use was found for all the blankets in camp, even with the camp fire. Nothing however disturbed our slumbers except a small animal of some kind in the lunch box. No "enchanted spirits" made themselves known, and they surely would have done so if they had been there, for no white man had ever slept there before. The descent was made in less than an hour with but little difficulty, and I wish it might be the pleasure of all who are interested in the past and this southwest wonderland, to see Katzimo, "the noblest single rock in America," as Mr. Charles F. Lummis has well called it.

Mesa Encantada, the summit

PLATES

Avalon Harbor, Catalina Island, 1895 37

38   *Tournament of Roses, Pasadena, 1895*

Tournament of Roses, the Pickwick Club, Pasadena, 1900   39

The Old Mill, Pasadena, 1895

In the Arroyo Seco, Pasadena, 1900   41

The Old Spanish Custom House, Monterey, California, 1897

The Camulos Rancho, south veranda, 1895   43

44   *The Camulos Rancho, the raised platform, 1895*

The Camulos Rancho, the fountain from the east, 1895   45

46   *The Guajome Rancho, the inner court veranda, 1896*

Yosemite Valley, from Inspiration Point, 1901   47

48   *Yosemite, the "General Grant" tree, 1901*

Yosemite, on the Wawona road, 1901   49

50   *Yosemite, the Merced River, 1901*

Yosemite Falls from the hotel, Hutchin's cabin, 1901   51

52   *Yosemite, Mirror Lake and Mt. Watkins, 1901*

Yosemite, Vernal Falls, 1901　　53

54   *Yosemite, Gipson the hermit, 1901*

Yosemite, Old Mary, 1901   55

56   *San Fernando Mission, the old palms, 1900*

San Luis Rey Mission, front of the chapel, 1897   57

58 *San Luis Rey Mission, baptistry, 1897*

San Luis Rey Mission, tule houses of Mission Indians, 1897 59

San Luis Rey Mission, entrance to the inner court, 1897

San Juan Capistrano Mission, The Very Reverend Father O'Keefe
in the inner court, 1900   61

San Gabriel Mission, the bells, 1897

San Juan Capistrano Mission, "The Club," L. TO R.: *H. E. Hoopes,*
G. J. Kuhrts, A. C. Vroman, H. I. Chatfield, unidentified, 1900   63

64   *Santa Inez Mission, old relics, 1896*

San Miguel Mission, altar, 1896   65

66   *Santa Clara Mission, altar, 1896*

*Acoma, over the pueblo from the roof of the old church, Mesa
Encantada at right, 1904*   67

68 *Zuñi Pueblo, interior, 1897*

Zuñi Pueblo, the small plaza, 1897   69

Zuñi Pueblo, the turquoise driller, 1904

Ta-ay-a-llona, sacred mountain of the Zuñi, 1899

Ta-ay-a-llona, the great shrine, 1899

Hawthorne Ranch, clouds, 1902 73

On the way to Hopi towns, "something that happened on the trip,"
1901

Twin Buttes, 1895   75

76   *Hopi towns, Walpi from the northeast, 1897*

Hopi towns, along the east side of the first mesa, 1897   77

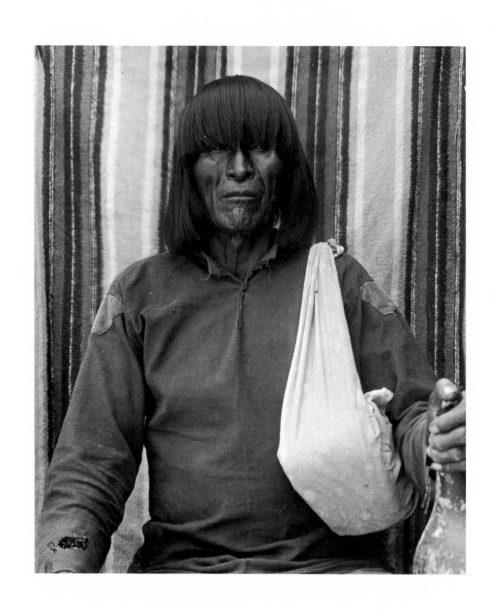

78   *Hopi portraits, Chief of Shipolovi, 1901*

Hopi towns, grinding corn, Tewa, 1895   79

80   *Hopi maiden with squash blossom hairdress, 1901*

Hopi towns, group of women and girls, Mishongnovi, 1898   81

82   *Hopi towns, blanket maker, Oraibi, 1902*

Hopi towns, Shipolovi and part of Mishongnovi from the rock east of Mishongnovi, 1902   83

84   *Hopi towns, madonna, 1901*

Hopi towns, "resting," Mishongnovi, 1898   85

86   *Hopi portraits, Nawquistewa, Oraibi, 1901*

Nampeyo, famous Hopi potter, 1901 87

Nampeyo firing her pottery, 1901

Hopi portraits, Nampeyo's daughter and baby, 1901   89

90   *Hopi towns, basket maker, 1900*

Hopi towns, cutting mutton, 1901   91

92   *Hopi portraits, Sekatila, 1901*

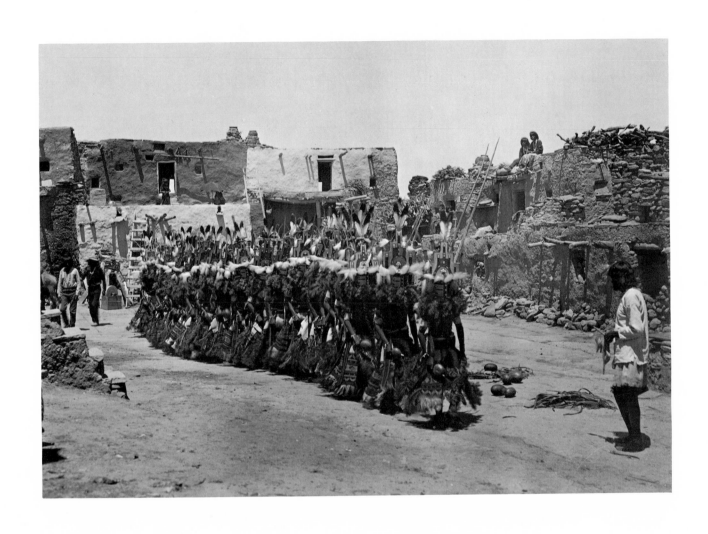

Hopi towns, the Niman dance, Shungopavi, 1901   93

94   *Curio room at Capt. Keams, Keams Canyon, Arizona, 1897*

Katchinatihu 95

96   *A street in Shungopavi, 1901*

Hopi towns, snake dance, Oraibi, 1898

98   *Hopi towns, snake dance, carrying the snakes, Oraibi, 1898*

Hopi towns, snake dance, purification ritual, Oraibi, 1898   99

100   *Hopi towns, snake priest, 1901*

Hopi towns, snake priest, 1901   101

102   *Hopi towns, snake priest, Mishongnovi, 1901*

Hopi portraits, Salako, snake priestess, 1901

104   *Hopi towns, one of the streets, Oraibi, 1898*

Hopi towns, men of Sichimovi, 1901   105

106   *Hopi towns, the man with a hoe, 1902*

Hopi portraits, Hahono, 1901   107

108   *Two Hopi maidens, 1898*

Hopi portraits, old Hopi man, 1900   109

110   *Hopi towns, hairdressing, 1901*

Santo Domingo church, New Mexico, 1899   111

112 *Mission, Santa Clara Pueblo, New Mexico, 1899*

Santa Fe, New Mexico, L. TO R.: *A. C. Vroman, Manuel Chaves,*
Dr. Elliott Coues, Amado Chaves, Frederick Webb Hodge,
George Parker Winship, 1899

114   *Cañon de Chelly, on the way up, 1904*

Cañon de Chelly, "more than a thousand feet!" 1904   115

116   *Cañon de Chelly, swastika or antelope ruin, 1904*

Cañon de Chelly, the White House Ruin, 1904   117

118   *Cañon de Chelly, Loco, Hubbell's cook, 1904*

Cañon de Chelly, in Mummy Cave, 1904   119

120   *Cañon de Chelly, A. C. Vroman, 1904*

Oregon, Illinois, Alligator Island on the Rock River, 1897   121

Media, Pennsylvania, country road with hay wagon, 1900

Media, Pennsylvania, haying, 1900

124   *Media, Pennsylvania, cow in stream, 1900*

Washington, D.C., the Library of Congress, interior, 1900   125

126   *Media, Pennsylvania, the old miller, 1900*

Media, Pennsylvania, old mill wheel, 1900